21st
Century
Skills Library

REAL WORLD MATH: GEOGRAPHY

ISLANDS

BY ANN HEINRICHS

Published in the United States of America by
Cherry Lake Publishing, Ann Arbor, Michigan
www.cherrylakepublishing.com

Content Adviser
Andrew Dombard, Associate Professor, Department of Earth and Environmental
Sciences, University of Illinois at Chicago
Math Adviser: Tonya Walker, MA, Boston University

Credits
Photos: Cover and page 1, ©lorga Studio, used under license from Shutterstock, Inc.;
page 4, ©imagebroker/Alamy; page 7, ©Stephen Aaron Rees, used under license
from Shutterstock, Inc.; page 9, ©Drimi, used under license from Shutterstock, Inc.;
page 10, ©Robert Harding Picture Library Ltd/Alamy; page 13, Marko Heuver, used
under license from Shutterstock, Inc.; page 14, ©AP Photo/Nome Nugget, Laurent
Dick; page 15, ©Arco Images GmbH/Alamy; page 16, ©iStockphoto.com/resonants;
pages 20 and 25, ©Ashley Cooper/Alamy; page 23, ©blickwinkel/Alamy; page 26,
©iStockphoto.com/pastorscott

Library of Congress Cataloging-in-Publication Data
Heinrichs, Ann.
  Islands / by Ann Heinrichs.
      p. cm.—(Real world math: geography)
  Includes index.
  ISBN-13: 978-1-60279-494-8
  ISBN-10: 1-60279-494-4
  1. Islands—Juvenile literature. I. Title.
  GB471.H45 2010
  551.42—dc22   2008054312

Cherry Lake Publishing would like to acknowledge
the work of The Partnership for 21st Century Skills.
Please visit *www.21stcenturyskills.org* for more information.

TABLE OF CONTENTS

CHAPTER ONE
WATER, WATER, EVERYWHERE

Teari dives for clams and octopus in the clear, blue waters. Erik creeps across the ice, stalking walruses. Misipeka climbs a palm tree to knock down some coconuts. These kids have at

The town of Sisimiut lies on the shores of Greenland which is the world's largest island.

least one thing in common. They all live on islands. This brings up an amazing math fact. About 10 percent of the world's population lives on islands. That's more than 600 million people!

An island is an area of land completely surrounded by water. That rule has only one exception. Continents, which are Earth's large landmasses, are not considered islands. It's easy to see why. The continents of North America and South America together may look like one gigantic island. The continent of Australia could be seen as a huge island, too. But these landmasses are so big that they don't count as true islands.

LIFE & CAREER SKILLS

Hurricane Wilma roared through the Florida Keys in October 2005. Hundreds of homes were flooded. As the storm approached, emergency agencies ordered residents of the Keys to leave their homes for safety. Fewer than 10 percent of the 78,000 residents left. They had grown tired of hurricane warnings. Would you have left? Suppose you were an emergency official during a hurricane. What would your concerns be?

REAL WORLD MATH CHALLENGE

Counting the end zones, a football field measures 120 yards long and 160 feet wide. **How many times would the island of Bishop Rock fit inside a football field?**

(Turn to page 29 for the answer)

You can learn some awesome math facts about islands. Islands come in a wide range of sizes. For example, the world's largest island is Greenland. It lies in the frigid waters northeast of Canada. Greenland covers about 836,331 square miles (2,166,087 square kilometers). That's more than three times the size of Texas!

Small islands are called islets, keys, or cays. The Florida Keys are a group of about 1,700 small islands. They stretch out from the southern tip of Florida. Bishop Rock is the world's smallest island with a building on it. It's a big rock off the coast of England with a lighthouse standing on it. The island measures 151 feet (46 meters) by 52 feet (16 m). That's about one-sixth the size of a soccer field!

Many lakes have islands in them. About 35,000 islands are scattered throughout the Great Lakes of the United States and Canada. Manitoulin Island, in Lake Huron, is the world's largest lake island. It covers 1,068 square miles (2,766 sq km).

The lighthouse on Bishop Rock was first lit in 1858.

That's big enough to hold all the dry land in the state of Rhode Island!

Have you ever covered your salad with Thousand Island dressing? It's named for a group of islands in the Saint Lawrence River. This river forms part of the border between Canada and New York State. There are actually 1,793 islands in this group. This number is based on three conditions geographers decided on for an island to be counted. It had to be above water all year long. It had to be bigger than 1 square foot (929 square centimeters). And it had to support at least one living tree!

Most of the world's islands are in the oceans. They come in all shapes and sizes. Many were formed in surprising ways. Let's see how math facts help tell their stories.

The Ivy Lea Bridge is part of the Thousand Islands bridge system that crosses the Saint Lawrence River and connects U.S. and Canadian highways.

CHAPTER TWO
CONTINENTAL AND VOLCANIC ISLANDS

Some islands used to be connected by land to a continent. Over time, ocean water covered part of the land, separating it from the rest of the mainland. An island formed

Oahu is the third-largest Hawaiian Island.

this way is called a **continental island**. Take the island of Tasmania, for example. It was once joined to the continent of Australia. The two began to separate about 10,000 years ago. Today, they're about 150 miles (241 km) apart.

Something different happened to Madagascar. It's an island off the east coast of Africa. Millions of years ago, Madagascar was part of the **supercontinent** of Gondwana. On one side, it was connected to today's Kenya, an African country. On the other side was India, now on the Asian continent. By about 90 million years ago, these landmasses had broken apart. Now Madagascar is the fourth-largest island in the world.

Most islands in the oceans are **volcanic** islands. They were formed by volcanoes erupting from the ocean floor. Over time, the **lava** kept building up and cooling. Finally, the land formed from the built-up lava broke through the ocean's surface.

The state of Hawaii is made up of hundreds of volcanic islands. They stretch more than 1,500 miles (2,414 km) through the Pacific Ocean. Of the eight main islands, the largest is Hawaii Island. Called the Big Island, it's the largest island in the United States.

Iceland is an island nation in the North Atlantic Ocean. People there live with more than just cold and ice. Iceland has hot features, too. It has several active volcanoes and many hot water springs. It also has geysers, or streams of hot water and steam that spew out of the ground. Iceland's offshore island of Surtsey is one of the youngest islands in the world. It emerged from the sea in the 1960s when an underwater volcano erupted.

21ST CENTURY CONTENT

About 87 percent of Iceland's buildings use **geothermal** power for their heat and hot water. Some Icelandic cities even heat their sidewalks during the winter! The United States produces more geothermal energy than any country in the world. But geothermal power provides less than 1 percent of U.S. electricity needs. Why do you think the United States doesn't make more use of its geothermal resources?

The Diomedes are a pair of volcanic islands. On the west is Big Diomede. It belongs to Russia, which is in Asia. Little Diomede, to the east, is part of Alaska. The two islands are only about 2.5 miles (4 km) apart. In the winter, when the water freezes, people can walk from one island to the other!

Steam and water shoot up from an Icelandic geyser.

Whoever makes this icy stroll is changing days. The **International Date Line** (IDL) passes between the Diomedes. This imaginary line marks the place where one calendar day changes to the previous or next calendar day. If it's noon and you cross the line from east to west, it becomes noon tomorrow. If you cross from west to east, you move from today to yesterday. This mind-boggling concept gave the Diomedes their nicknames. Big Diomede is called Tomorrow Island, and Little Diomede is called Yesterday Isle!

Young skiers head back to Little Diomede across the frozen Bering Strait. Big Diomede can be seen behind them.

A ship sails past Big Diomede.

REAL WORLD MATH CHALLENGE

Kiri and Tana live on two separate Pacific Islands that are 8¼ miles apart. Kiri's island is west of the International Date Line, and Tana's island is east of it. Tana is having a birthday party at 3:00 P.M., and Kiri plans to row her canoe there. She can row 3 miles per hour. **If she leaves her island at noon that day, how long before the party will she arrive?**

(Turn to page 29 for the answer)

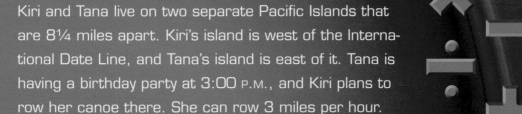

CHAPTER THREE

DO THE MATH: ARCHIPELAGOS, ATOLLS, AND BARRIER ISLANDS

A cluster or chain of islands is called an **archipelago**. Many entire countries are archipelagos. For example, Japan is an archipelago with more than 3,900 islands.

The Stockholm Archipelago is located along the coast of Stockholm, the capital city of Sweden.

Mount Fuji, Japan's highest peak, is an active volcano. No one worries about it much, though. It hasn't erupted since 1707.

Indonesia is the world's largest archipelago nation. It's in Southeast Asia, between the Asian mainland and Australia. Indonesia has about 18,000 islands, with a total area of 735,355 square miles (1.9 million sq km). But people live on only about 6,000 of those islands.

Some islands are made of tiny sea creatures called coral polyps. They grow a hard skeleton on the outside of their bodies. As old polyps die, new polyps build up on top of the old ones. Eventually, they form a hardened, rocklike mass. Such a mass in shallow water is called a **coral reef**. If a reef emerges above the ocean's surface, it becomes a coral island.

21ST CENTURY CONTENT

Tokyo is Japan's capital city. About 35 million people live in its metropolitan area. That's the built-up area extending out from the city. Tokyo is an example of what's called an urban heat island. This means it's warmer than surrounding areas because of its high population. Why do you think this happens?

The world's largest coral reef system is the Great Barrier Reef, along the northeastern coast of Australia. It's made up of about 3,400 reefs and 300 coral islands. The Great Barrier Reef extends for about 1,250 miles (2,000 km) through the ocean. It's so big that astronauts can see it from space!

Coral often builds up around the fringes of a volcanic island. Over time, wind and waves wash the island away. But the coral keeps growing. This creates an **atoll**, a ring of coral islands around a shallow **lagoon**. The world's largest chain of atolls is the Tuamotu Islands. Its 78 coral atolls spread across more than 330 square miles (855 sq km) of the Pacific Ocean.

REAL WORLD MATH CHALLENGE

Tikehau is an atoll in the Tuamotu group. Its lagoon is 17 miles long and 12 miles wide. Canoe A crosses the lagoon the long way at 5 ¾ miles per hour. Canoe B paddles across the short way at 4 ¼ miles per hour. **If both canoes start out at the same time, which one will reach the opposite side of the lagoon first?**

(Turn to page 29 for the answer)

Barrier islands are long, narrow islands that build up along a coastline. They are composed mostly of sand. The world's longest barrier island is Padre Island, measuring about 130 miles (209 km) long. It lies off the coast of Texas in the Gulf of Mexico.

The Outer Banks is a 200-mile (322 km) string of barrier islands off the coast of North Carolina. The famous pirate Blackbeard used to hide out on the Outer Banks. He used math to calculate how close a ship must be before he could rob it!

REAL WORLD MATH CHALLENGE

David has a map for Blackbeard the pirate's buried treasure on the Outer Banks. He wants to find the treasure. The **map scale** says ¼ inch = 5 miles. First, David has to travel from his home to the North Carolina coast. On the map, that's 7 inches. A boat from the coast to the Outer Banks' shore is 1½ inches. Then it's another ¼ inch to the treasure. **How far does David travel on his treasure hunt?**

(Turn to page 29 for the answer)

CHAPTER FOUR
DO THE MATH: DISAPPEARING ISLANDS

Kids in Tuvalu play on the trunks of fallen palm trees. Sometimes they wade through ankle-deep water on their way to school. They don't realize their island home is shrinking.

Rising tides can cause serious damage to the islands of Tuvalu.

Tuvalu is a nation of nine tiny coral islands in the Pacific Ocean. They're about halfway between Hawaii and Australia. When the daily ocean **tides** rise, most of Tuvalu is just 3 feet (1 m) above water. Sand washes away from the beaches, and palm trees topple over on the shore.

Islanders around the world worry about their homelands shrinking. Many scientists believe the shrinking is due to climate change. As temperatures grow warmer, ocean levels rise. Warmer temperatures make Earth's ice melt. They also make the ocean waters expand to take up more space. A team of scientists studied this problem for the United Nations in 2007. They predicted that sea levels would rise 7 to 23 inches (18 to 58 cm) by the end of the 21st century.

REAL WORLD MATH CHALLENGE

Many Tuvalu villagers build their homes on stilts 3 feet above ground. The highest tides rise 11 feet. Tuvalu's highest point is 16 feet above sea level. **If a hut were built on the highest point, how close to the hut's floor would the highest tides reach?**

(Turn to page 29 for the answer)

Many islands are also undergoing **erosion**. Waves batter their shores, sweeping sand and soil away. Some coral islands sit atop volcanic rock that's sinking. Like Tuvalu, these islands are slowly disappearing. Here are some of their stories.

Kiribati is a nation of 32 atolls in the Pacific Ocean. About 110,000 people live there. Kiribati's average elevation is about 6 feet (1.8 m). In 1999, two islands in one of Kiribati's atolls, Tarawa, disappeared under water. Dozens of families on the atoll have moved to higher ground.

LEARNING & INNOVATION SKILLS

Mohamed Nasheed, president of the Maldives, believes his nation's entire population should move. He wants to purchase a new homeland for them. Possible locations are in Sri Lanka, India, and Australia. In the past, Maldivians have tried to save their land by building seawalls and artificial islands. But Nasheed says these solutions are too expensive to work on a large scale. What are some of the pluses and minuses of Nasheed's plan?

The people of the Maldives must pay close attention to rising water levels.

The Maldives is an island country south of India. It's a chain of 1,192 coral islands grouped into 26 atolls. About 370,000 people make their homes on 200 of those islands. The Maldives is the lowest country in the world. Its average elevation is only 4.9 feet (1.5 m) above sea level. Geographers plan to redraw maps of the Maldives because they are shrinking so much.

People on the Carteret Islands are packing up and leaving. These islands belong to Papua New Guinea, a country northeast of Australia. Seawater is washing away the islanders' homes and drowning their vegetable gardens. The islands are expected to disappear completely by 2015. In 2009, the government began slowly relocating the entire population of the Carterets to nearby Bougainville Island. That means moving about 2,000 people! Many lifelong residents refuse to leave, though. They say they'd rather sink with the islands.

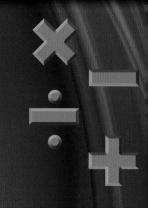

REAL WORLD MATH CHALLENGE

Carteret Islanders are being moved from 2009 to 2014. But one-third of the islands' 2,000 people don't want to leave. **Of the two-thirds who want to move, what's the average number of people who must leave every year?** Answer with the nearest whole number.

(Turn to page 29 for the answer)

Many island homes are endangered by rising waters due to global climate change.

CHAPTER FIVE
NO MAN IS AN ISLAND

Why do we care about islands? For one thing, they're great places to have fun. Thousands of families visit islands every year. They enjoy the beaches, splash in the waves, and explore coral reefs. Math comes in handy on island vacations. Using map scales, visitors can figure out the distance to an island and the time it will take to reach it. With math facts about tides and sea levels, they can plan for a safe visit.

Many island beaches are popular vacation spots.

Islands offer much more than fun. They give us food, too. Islanders harvest coconuts, pineapples, and other foods. They export those products to other countries. Many islanders also make their living by fishing. They provide much of the seafood we eat.

Using math, we can study trends in island fishing. This gives us valuable information about our food supplies. For example, people on Canada's island of Newfoundland have depended on fishing for centuries. Newfoundlanders caught 810,000 tons of cod in 1968. But by 2001, the yearly catch was only about 7,000 tons. The supply of cod was almost fished out. There weren't as many cod in the water for the fishermen to catch. Many other island fishers report shrinking catches, too.

Islands are also good locations for studying climate change. Using math, we can gather information about islands' sea levels, beach erosion, and melting ice. These factors are at work on the coastlines of our continents, too.

In the 1600s, the poet John Donne wrote, "No man is an island." He meant we are all connected. Whatever happens to one person affects us all. In a way, no island is an island, either. Whatever happens to Earth's islands affects the world community. You may not live on an island, but 600 million other people do. You can easily connect with their everyday problems and ways of life. Just do the math!

21ST CENTURY CONTENT

Banks Island is in Canada's far-northern Arctic region. Most of its residents are Inuit people. They have begun to see robins, mosquitoes, and sand flies around their homes. Common in warmer areas, these species are new to Banks Island. Ice around the island used to be thick and solid, but it has grown thin. Both hunters and caribou have fallen through the ice and died. In 1998, islanders started a community project called Inuit Observations on Climate Change. They hope it will help inform others about the effects of global warming. What changes do you think Banks Islanders are making in their traditional lifestyles?

REAL WORLD MATH CHALLENGE ANSWERS

Chapter One

Page 6
The island of Bishop Rock could fit inside a football field 7 times.
120 yards x 3 feet = 360 feet
Area of football field: 360 feet x 160 feet = 57,600 square feet
Area of Bishop Rock: 151 feet x 52 feet = 7,852 square feet
57,600 square feet ÷ 7,852 square feet = 7.335 = 7 times

Chapter Two

Page 15
Kiri will arrive 24 hours and 15 minutes before the party.
8.25 mi ÷ 3 mph = 2.75 hours
Noon + 2.75 hours = 2:45 P.M.
3:00 P.M. – 2:45 P.M. = 15 minutes
Kiri crosses the IDL so she arrives 24 hours earlier.
15 min + 24 hours = 24 hours and 15 minutes

Chapter Three

Page 18
Canoe B will reach the other side of the lagoon first.
Canoe A travels 17 miles.
17 mi ÷ 5.75 mph = 2.96 hours
Canoe B travels 12 miles.
12 miles ÷ 4.25 miles per hour = 2.82 hours

Page 19
David has to travel 175 miles.
Home to the North Carolina coast:

7 in ÷ ¼ in = 7 x 4 = 28 in
28 in x 5 mi = 140 mi
Coast to the Outer Banks' shore:
1½ in ÷ ¼ in = 1.5 x 4 = 6 in
6 in x 5 mi = 30 mi
To the treasure:
¼ in ÷ ¼ in = 0.25 x 4 = 1 in
1 in x 5 mi = 5 mi
140 mi + 30 mi + 5 mi = 175 mi

Chapter Four

Page 21
The highest tides would reach 8 feet from the hut's floor.
16 feet + 3 feet = 19 feet
19 feet – 11 feet = 8 feet

Page 24
Of those who have agreed to move, 267 people must leave every year.
$\frac{2}{3}$ of the people agree to move:
$1 - \frac{1}{3} = \frac{2}{3}$
$\frac{2}{3}$ x 2,000 = 1,333.33 people
2014 – 2009 = 5 years
1,333.33 people ÷ 5 years = 266.67, or 267 people per year

Chapter Five

Page 27
About 28% of the world's tuna comes from the Pacific Islands region.
1 million tons ÷ 3.6 million tons = 0.277
0.277 = 28%

GLOSSARY

archipelago (ar-kuh-PEL-uh-goh) a cluster or chain of islands

atoll (A-tol) a ring of coral islands

barrier islands (BA-ree-ur EYE-luhndz) long, narrow, sandy islands that build up along a coastline

continental island (kon-tuh-NEN-tuhl EYE-luhnd) an island once connected by land to a continent

coral reef (KOR-uhl REEF) a rocklike structure composed of coral that has built up over many years

erosion (ih-ROH-zhuhn) a process in which wind, water, or ice wear away land or soil

geothermal (gee-oh-THUR-muhl) related to heat coming from deep within the earth

International Date Line (in-tur-NASH-uh-nuhl DAYT LINE) an imaginary line at 180° longitude where one calendar day changes to the previous or next calendar day

lagoon (luh-GOON) a body of shallow water separated from deeper ocean waters

lava (LAH-vuh) hot, melted rock emitted by a volcano

map scale (MAP SKAYL) a note or symbol on a map telling the relation between distances on the map and real-world distances

supercontinent (SOO-pur-kon-tuh-nent) a huge landmass made up of more than one present-day continent

tides (TIDEZ) the regular rise and fall of the ocean's surface

volcanic (vol-KA-nihk) related to volcanoes

FOR MORE INFORMATION

BOOKS

Gibbons, Gail. *Surrounded by Sea: Life on a New England Fishing Island*. New York: Holiday House, 2005.

Green, Jen. *Islands Around the World*. New York: PowerKids Press, 2009.

Mis, Melody S. *Exploring Islands*. New York: PowerKids Press, 2009.

WEB SITES

Conservation International: Pacific Islands

www.conservation.org/explore/regions/asia-pacific/pacific_islands/Pages/overview.aspx
To find out about the land, wildlife, and environment of several Pacific island groups

How Barrier Islands Work

science.howstuffworks.com/barrier-island.htm
All about barrier islands, how they were formed, and how they are changing

The Nature Conservancy: Islands

www.nature.org/wherewework/islands/
Information about environmental issues and unique animals of many islands around the world

INDEX

ABOUT THE AUTHOR

Ann Heinrichs has traveled through Africa, the Middle East, East Asia, Europe, and North America. She has written more than 200 books for children and young adults on U.S. and world geography, history, and culture. Ann grew up in Fort Smith, Arkansas, and now lives in Chicago, Illinois. When she's not traveling, she enjoys kayaking and bicycling.